Engineering Marvels

MUSCLE CARS

Graphs, Tables, and Equations

Elisa Jordan, M.A.

Contributing Author

Alison S. Marzocchi, Ph.D.

Consultants

Colleen Pollitt, M.A.Ed.
Math Support Teacher
Howard County Public Schools

Gene Jordan

Publishing Credits

Rachelle Cracchiolo, M.S.Ed., *Publisher*
Conni Medina, M.A.Ed., *Editor in Chief*
Dona Herweck Rice, *Series Developer*
Emily R. Smith, M.A.Ed., *Series Developer*
Diana Kenney, M.A.Ed., NBCT, *Content Director*
Stacy Monsman, M.A., *Editor*
Michelle Jovin, M.A., *Associate Editor*
Kevin Panter, *Senior Graphic Designer*

Image Credits: front cover, p.1 Janek Sergejev/Shutterstock; p.6 (top), p.8 Everett Collection/Shutterstock; p.6 (second from top) Library of Congress [LC-USZ62-118659], Library of Congress [LC-USZ62-62286]; p.6 (middle) Library of Congress [LC-USZ62-44478]; p.6 (fourth from top) Library of Congress [LC-USE6-D-009119]; p.6 (bottom) Kirn Vintage Stock/Corbis via Getty Images; p.9 (top) Philip Pilosian/Shutterstock; p.9 (bottom right) SergBob/Shutterstock; p.9 (bottom left) Kevin M. McCarthy/Shutterstock; p.10 (middle) Leena Robinson/Shutterstock; p.10 (bottom) Betto Rodrigues/Shutterstock; p.11 (top) Steve Lagreca/Shutterstock; p.13 (center left) Marvin McAbee/Alamy; p.13 (center right) Lloyd Carr/Shutterstock; p.13 (bottom) Greg Gjerdingen; p.15 (all) BoJack/Shutterstock; p.16 Sicnag/Flickr; p.18 Steve Lagreca/Shutterstock; p.19 (top) Barry Blackburn/Shutterstock; p.19 (bottom) Philip Pilosian/Shutterstock; p.20 allanw/Shutterstock; p.22, 23 (top right) Michael Ochs Archives/Getty Images; p.23 (bottom) Gertan/Shutterstock; p.24 Grzegorz Czapski/Shutterstock; p.25 (top) Magnus Manske; p.25 (bottom) Performance Image/Alamy; p.27 (top) Jeremy Warner/iStock; p.27 (bottom) Tramino/iStock; p.29 Art Konovalov/Shutterstock; all other images from iStock and/or Shutterstock.

Library of Congress Cataloging-in-Publication Data

Names: Jordan, Elisa, author.
Title: Muscle cars : graphs, tables, and equations / Elisa Jordan, M.A.
Description: Huntington Beach, CA : Teacher Created Materials, Inc., [2019] | Series: Engineering marvels | Includes bibliographical references and index. | Audience: Grades 4 to 6. |
Identifiers: LCCN 2018051877 (print) | LCCN 2018055003 (ebook) | ISBN 9781425855321 (eBook) | ISBN 9781425858889 (pbk. : alk. paper)
Subjects: LCSH: Muscle cars—Juvenile literature.
Classification: LCC TL147 (ebook) | LCC TL147 .J673 2019 (print) | DDC 629.222—dc23
LC record available at https://lccn.loc.gov/2018051877

We at Teacher Created Materials would like to thank Susan and Bert Jovin for their time and expertise in making this reader possible.

Teacher Created Materials

5301 Oceanus Drive
Huntington Beach, CA 92649-1030
www.tcmpub.com

ISBN 978-1-4258-5888-9

© 2019 Teacher Created Materials, Inc.
Printed in Malaysia
Thumbprints.21254

Table of Contents

Introducing Muscle Cars! 4

Setting the Stage 6

Taking the World by Storm 16

Muscle Car Culture 22

A Lasting Impact 26

Problem Solving 28

Glossary 30

Index 31

Answer Key 32

Introducing Muscle Cars!

As soon as motorcars took the place of horses and carriages, engineers started working to improve them. People like good-looking cars. They also like cars that can get them places faster. That's where muscle cars come in!

People have loved muscle cars from the beginning. There was something really special about them. The engines had a lot of power. That, combined with a lightweight body, made them superfast. Some people tested that speed by racing them on streets or on **drag strips**. In fact, they were so much fun that car enthusiasts still love them!

Muscle cars were so popular that an entire **car culture** sprang up around them. Music, movies, and television reflected Americans' love for these cars.

The muscle car era was primarily from 1964 to the early 1970s, but they left a legacy in the car world. The influence of muscle cars is still felt in the United States and in other parts of the world. Their impact evolved into one of the most memorable car eras of all time!

The Ford Mustang is a popular muscle car that is still in production. The graph shows the number of Mustangs produced each year during the muscle car era.

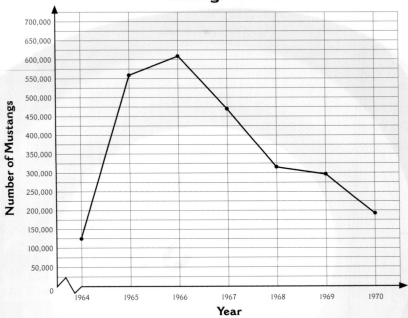

Mustangs Produced

1. What are the independent and dependent variables?

2. Describe the data by completing the sentence frame: During the muscle car era, the number of Mustangs _____.

Setting the Stage

Originally, people got around on horseback or with horse-drawn carriages. By the early 1900s, the idea of horseless carriages—cars—was becoming popular. They were easy to use. However, they were expensive. This was because cars were made one at a time. A man named Henry Ford set out to change that.

Ford set up the first **assembly line** for cars. This allowed cars to be made quickly and inexpensively. Ford's car was called the Model-T. It was considered the first affordable motor vehicle. From that point, Americans fell in love with cars. They came in all shapes and sizes. But in the early 1940s, production of passenger vehicles was halted. World War II forced automakers to **repurpose** themselves as they made things needed for the war, such as tanks and airplanes.

When the war ended in 1945, people were thrilled. The United States was on the winning side. Families were buying houses that were springing up in newly built suburbs. So many babies were born over the next few years that there was a **baby boom**. It was a **prosperous** time, and Americans were excited to buy cars again.

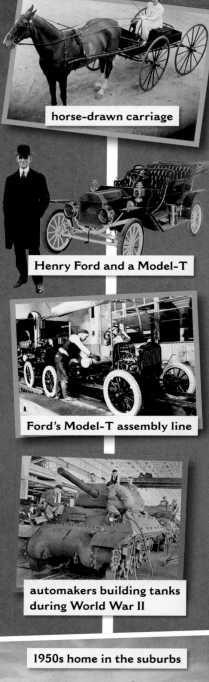

horse-drawn carriage

Henry Ford and a Model-T

Ford's Model-T assembly line

automakers building tanks during World War II

1950s home in the suburbs

The graph shows the approximate percent of households in the United States that owned cars.

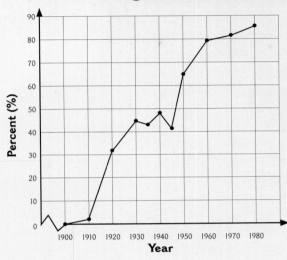

Car-Owning U.S. Households

1. What does the ordered pair (1900, 0) mean?

2. What does it mean when the line on the graph goes down?

3. Write the data from this graph in a table like this one.

Year	Percent (%)
1900	
1910	
1920	
1930	
1940	
1950	
1960	
1970	
1980	

4. What is an advantage of displaying this data as a graph instead of a table?

The Big Three and Big Changes

After the war, the car industry played a big role in the recovery of the United States' economy. There were three major auto companies producing most of the cars in the country. They were known as the Big Three—Ford Motor Company, Chrysler, and General Motors (GM). All three were located in the city of Detroit.

Detroit

The Big Three provided Americans with lots and lots of cars. Car sales doubled by the end of the 1950s. The Big Three also created many jobs. At that time, the car **industry** employed about one in six working Americans.

Engineers for the Big Three worked to make cars better. They made cars with new options, such as power steering and automatic **transmissions**. Cars became safer too, as some began to have seat belts and power brakes.

Cars also got a new look. Travel and space were popular themes in the 1950s. Airplanes, rockets, and trains influenced car body shapes. Cars became wider and longer.

But by far, the biggest cultural impact came from the engines.

1950s Ford cars are checked by workers before being sold.

This 1956 Chevy Bel Air was produced by GM.

LET'S EXPLORE MATH

Car sales doubled by the end of the 1950s. Use b to stand for the number of cars sold before the end of the decade and a to stand for the number of cars sold at the end of the decade. Choose all the equations that show how the variables are related.

A. $a = 2b$ **B.** $b = 2a$ **C.** $a = \frac{1}{2}b$ **D.** $b = \frac{1}{2}a$

This 1955 Chevy hood ornament was designed to look like an airplane.

1957 Chevy engine

Big, Flashy, and Lots of Engine!

One of the biggest changes in engines was the **overhead valve V8 engine**. They became common in the 1950s. The V8 engine gave cars more power to accelerate quicker and go faster.

For example, the 1949 Oldsmobile Rocket 88 had a V8 engine and a two-barrel **carburetor**. A carburetor blends the air and fuel in the engine. The Rocket also had 135 **horsepower**, so it was fast! It was a whole new type of car. And it looked cool. The cars had long engine hoods, and buyers could choose between two- or four-door models. Cars evolved over the years, so there is no "first" muscle car. But the Rocket 88 was definitely one of the original muscle cars.

1949 Oldsmobile Rocket 88

Rocket 88 V8 engine

1955 Chrysler C-300

The 1955 Chrysler C-300 was the first car to have 300 horsepower as a standard feature. That was a lot of horsepower. Going fast had just gotten easier!

The 1950s was a time of great joy, and that was reflected in cars. They had fast and powerful engines. Many of them had large fins in back, a lot of chrome, and fancy taillights. But the best was yet to come!

1950s Cadillac tail fin

The Importance of the Engine

Muscle cars got their name from their powerful engines. Gas-powered muscle cars had **internal combustion engines** (ICE). ICEs are still used in gas cars. First, a fuel and air mixture goes into a cylinder. Then, a **piston** compresses the mixture. The spark plug creates a spark. The spark causes an explosion when it hits the fuel, which pushes the piston down. When the piston comes back up, it forces out exhaust. Pipes take this exhaust (burned gas) away from the engine and the driver. Exhaust leaves the car through an exhaust pipe and the process begins again.

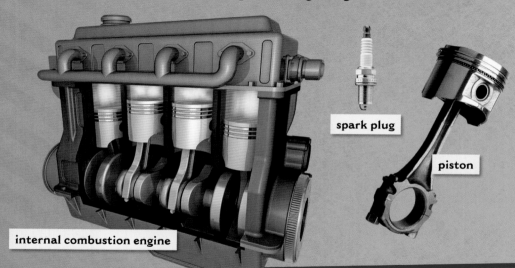

spark plug

piston

internal combustion engine

1 Fuel and air mixture goes into the cylinder.

2 A piston compresses the mixture.

3 The spark plug causes an explosion, pushing the piston down.

4 The piston rises again and pushes out exhaust.

Muscle car engines are very powerful. In addition to increased horsepower, cubic inches are often mentioned when it comes to engines. An engine's cubic inches is the volume that pistons take up in the cylinders, as the pistons move up and down. Take the Chevy Impala 409 as an example. It has an **engine displacement** of 409 cubic inches. The higher the number for cubic inches displaced, the more power a car has. Sometimes, this is coded into the car name, such as the 409.

Chevy Impala 409 engine

1963 Chevy Impala

Forces at Work

Torque and horsepower are major factors in an engine. They're related but different. Basically, torque gets things moving. Horsepower is the force that keeps them moving.

Torque causes rotation and forces an engine's **crankshaft** to turn. The crankshaft rotates in a circle. When engine displacement is increased, it creates more torque. So, when cars were made with larger displacement numbers, like the 409, they had a lot of torque, or power.

Horsepower was named after the amount of work a horse can do, but carmakers also use it to measure the power of engines. Horsepower tells buyers how much resistance an engine can handle. For muscle cars, the ideal resistance an engine can handle is 10 pounds to 1 horsepower.

The term "muscle car" has a simple formula. It basically means a larger engine in a smaller car body, typically a coupe. (A *coupe* has a hard roof and two doors.) Coupes are typically lighter, which makes them faster.

Muscle cars were ideal for street racing. Other times, races were set up in advance at drag strips so friends could watch. The excitement of speed and racing was a big part of why these cars were so popular.

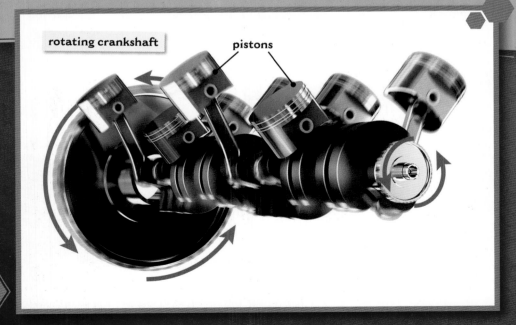

rotating crankshaft

pistons

A 1967 Ford Mustang GT coupe does a burnout.

The variables in each statement appear in italics. Describe what a graph for each situation would look like.

1. "The more *cubic inches displaced*, the more *power* a car has."

2. "When *engine displacement* is increased, it creates more *torque*."

A Dodge Dart races other classic muscle cars in 2018.

Taking the World by Storm

When the 1961 Chevy Impala SS (Super Sport) 409 arrived, GM knew it was special. It was different from any other car. It had a 409–cubic inch V8 engine and 360 horsepower. The engine was huge, and it was also seriously powerful. But it was more than just a bigger engine. Stronger **shocks** kept the car from bouncing too much. It had forged aluminum pistons, which are ideal for high-performance cars. These pistons stood up better to extreme heat and allowed engines to produce more power. The car's power brakes had metallic linings, which made them last longer and make quick stops faster.

The Impala SS's body looked good too. It was a long, sleek coupe with chrome stripes. The chrome provided a small strip for a second color to pop and contrast with the main body. The wheels had white walls. Inside, there was a padded dash and a grab bar on the glove box so passengers could hold on while drivers sped along.

Because the 409 was such a new type of car, not many were made, but word spread fast and their reputation grew. In 1962, the band The Beach Boys released a song about the "real fine" 409, and the car quickly became a legend.

1961 Chevy Impala SS 409

A 1961 Chevrolet Impala SS 409 had 360 horsepower. At top speed during tests, it took about 14 seconds to travel $\frac{1}{4}$ (or quarter) mile. The table shows horsepower and quarter-mile times for other muscle cars.

Car	Horsepower	Quarter-Mile Time (seconds)
1964 Pontiac GTO	325	15.8
1967 Shelby Cobra 427	425	12.2
1969 Chevy Camaro ZL1	430	13.1
1969 Ford Mustang 428	365	14.3
1970 Chevrolet Chevelle SS	450	13.2

1. Plot points on a scatterplot like this one to show the relationship between horsepower and quarter-mile times.

Horsepower and Quarter-Mile Times for Muscle Cars

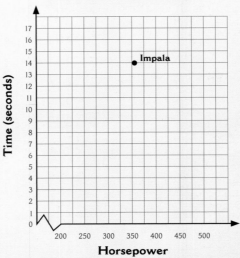

2. How can you describe the relationship between horsepower and quarter-mile times?

Pontiac GTO

The car world changed again in 1964. That's when GM released the Pontiac GTO, and muscle cars officially became a trend. You could get different engine sizes for the GTO, but one option was a 389 cubic-inch V8 engine. Another option was called a "tri-power engine."

The regular V8 engine could go 0–60 miles (about 0–100 kilometers) per hour in around 7 seconds. With the tri-power engine, it took less than 6 seconds. The tri-power option got its speed from having two additional carburetors over the V8's single-carburetor setup.

GTOs were specially designed for speed and power. They were almost like race cars for the streets. Like the 409, the body style was a longer coupe. GTOs were considered the ultimate fun car.

Their impact on American culture was huge. Popular music groups began singing about GTOs. Ronny & the Daytonas sang "Little GTO," and the lyrics had details about the engine. Jan and Dean, a favorite duo among teens, sang "My Mighty GTO." Songwriters Carol & Cheryl wrote and sang "Go Go GTO" in 1965.

The GTO had a huge impact on the car industry. After its success, the Big Three carmakers in Detroit began investing heavily in muscle cars.

1966 Pontiac GTO

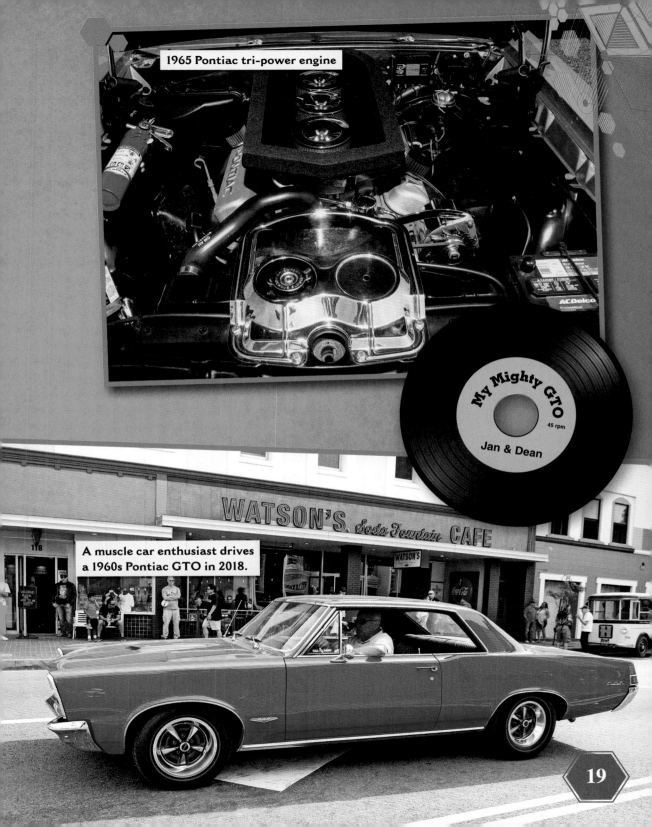

1965 Pontiac tri-power engine

My Mighty GTO
45 rpm
Jan & Dean

A muscle car enthusiast drives a 1960s Pontiac GTO in 2018.

The Party's Over

By the 1970s, muscle cars were decreasing in popularity. Gas prices increased, and insurance companies charged more money to cover muscle cars.

They were also bad for air quality. The government told car companies to decrease **emissions**. Safety standards were also updated for all cars, and bumpers got bigger to provide more protection in crashes. That added extra weight. These changes slowed cars down.

A few muscle cars survived, like Pontiac's Trans Am. The Trans Am was featured in the movie *Smokey and the Bandit*. The car's success was rare. Most of the other muscle cars were gone. But many people missed them. Car engineers thought about how to bring them back.

Starting in the 1980s, better technology meant cars could be built with electronic fuel injection (EFI). EFI was more precise than carburetors were. The correct mix of fuel and air is essential for a car to run efficiently. EFI performs this function well and is still used.

There were many benefits to this change. Engines became more reliable and used less gas. An added bonus was fewer emissions, so the air wasn't as dirty. Muscle cars were back!

1979 Pontiac Trans Am

During the 1960s, a gallon of gas cost about $0.32. But gas prices increased during the 1970s. This increase was one of the reasons muscle cars decreased in popularity.

1. Draw a table like this one. Use the information to track the cost of gas in 1971, 1976, and 1981.

Number of Gallons of Gas	Cost ($)		
	1971	1976	1981
0	0	0	0
2	0.72		
4		2.36	
6			7.86
8			
10			
12			

2. Set up a graph like this one. Plot the data for each year. Remember to write labels for the independent and dependent variables, and to make a key to identify the lines representing each year.

Cost of Gas

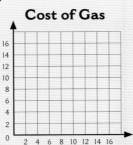

3. What does 1 gallon of gas cost each year?

4. Write an equation for each year that shows the relationship between the number of gallons of gas and cost. Use n to stand for the number of gallons of gas and c to stand for cost.

21

Muscle Car Culture

Muscle cars symbolized the spirit of the 1960s. This included freedom, rebellion, and status. Songs about them were popular. They showed what it was like to drive muscle cars.

Starting back in 1950, one of the first rock 'n' roll songs was called "Rocket 88," after one of the first muscle-type cars. Music's obsession with fast cars continued.

The Beach Boys sang "409" and "Shut Down," which was about a drag race. Jan and Dean sang about "The Little Old Lady from Pasadena." That was a funny song about an old lady driving her Dodge really fast. They also sang "Dead Man's Curve," about a real-life street racing accident in Los Angeles. Another popular song was "Mustang Sally." The rhythm-and-blues song was about a girl obsessed with her Ford Mustang.

Muscle cars continued to inspire people over the years. In 1978, Bruce Springsteen wrote a song called "Racing in the Street" about a 1969 Chevy. Then, there's "Mercury Blues." First written in 1949 as "Mercury Boogie," it's been redone four times! The song was a tribute to the Mercury Eight car.

The Beach Boys perform in 1964.

Wilson Pickett popularized "Mustang Sally" in 1966.

ATLANTIC
45 R.P.M.
45-2365
VOCAL
Pub. Fourteenth
Hour, BMI
Time: 3:03
MUSTANG SALLY
(Rice)
WILSON PICKETT
A-11028

1965 Ford Mustang convertible

Mustangs and Chargers

Muscle cars were so popular that movies celebrated them. One of the most famous was *Bullitt*, starring Steve McQueen. The green 1968 Mustang **fastback** was practically a character in the movie. There were awesome car chases between the Mustang and a 1968 Dodge Charger! In the Transformers movie series, Bumblebee starts out as an old 1977 Camaro.

There were a lot of popular muscle cars, but Ford Mustangs and Dodge Chargers stand out most. Mustang was introduced as Ford's answer to other fast coupes hitting the road. Unlike the 409 and GTO, the Mustang had a shorter body. It also had raised vents on the sides (called "scoops") that let air flow to the brakes to keep them cool.

Chargers remained popular with car buffs for years. They came out in 1966. By 1968, they were considered a high standard for muscle cars. They had fast engines, but no other cars looked like them. Chrome was minimal. They had elegant curved bodies. When the headlights were turned on, it looked like eyes opening. It's no wonder they were in movies. They had star quality!

1968 Mustang fastback

side scoop

1968 Dodge Charger

LET'S EXPLORE MATH

Today, a Mustang GT convertible costs about $14\frac{1}{2}$ times as much as a 1968 Mustang GT convertible did. Use p to stand for the cost in the past and t to stand for the cost today. Write an equation to show how the prices are related.

1968 Ford Mustang GT convertible

A Lasting Impact

Thanks to popular culture and improved technology, muscle cars are thriving again. Those who like the older cars can gather at shows where old muscle cars are displayed. Car lovers collect them. Many people fix them up so they run again. New paint and restored interiors bring cars back to their former glory.

modern V6 engine

Then, there is the new generation of muscle cars. People drive them every day. Many modern high-performance cars have V6 engines, which are more compact and cheaper to make than V8s. The V8 engine is more powerful but the V6 has better fuel consumption. That's still a pretty fast engine, and it's better for the environment.

The muscle car revival has been steady because technology keeps getting better. Automakers also understand that these cars need to look good. That's a big part of their appeal. Makers of newer high-performance cars took what people loved about older muscle cars and improved them. The new cars are a lot like the ones of yesterday. They still symbolize excitement and individuality. Old and new combine to make the new ideal muscle car!

A man and his granddaughter work on a 1960s Ford Mustang.

1968 Chevrolet Camaro

2016 Chevrolet Camaro

🎛️ Problem Solving

Imagine that you write for a website that provides information to muscle car enthusiasts. You answer questions that readers email you. You receive this email:

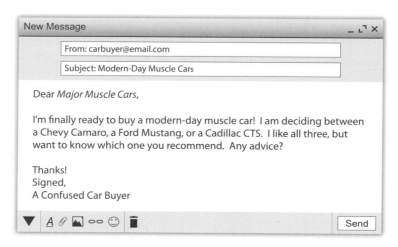

Use the table, equations, and fact sheets to write a response. Be sure to include information about base price, braking distance, and acceleration when making your recommendation. Also, provide the reader with a table and graph showing the depreciation of the recommended car over five years.

Car	Base Price ($)	Braking Distance (ft.)	0–60 Time (sec.)	Approximate Depreciation Equation
Chevy Camaro	25,905	116.2	3.7	$d = 1{,}497t + 3{,}847$
Ford Mustang	25,585	119.1	5.3	$d = 1{,}813t + 2{,}292$
Cadillac CTS	46,495	109	4.4	$d = 3{,}333t + 9{,}439$

Base Price

The *base price* is the starting cost of a car before adding extra features.

Braking Distance

The *braking distance* is how many feet it takes for a car to come to a full stop when drivers apply the brakes while traveling 60 miles per hour. Shorter braking distances are better because it means drivers can stop more quickly.

Acceleration

The *0–60 time* is how many seconds it takes for a car to reach 60 miles per hour from a full stop. A lower time is better because it means the car can accelerate quickly.

Depreciation

A car's value decreases with age. This is known as *depreciation*. A car that depreciates slowly is a better buy than a car that depreciates quickly because drivers won't lose as much money when they resell it. In the equations, t stands for time in years and d stands for total depreciation amount. The *depreciation amount* is how much money is deducted from the original cost of the car.

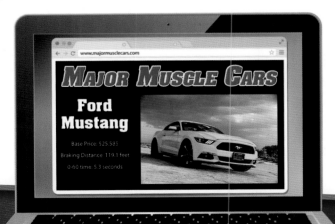

MAJOR MUSCLE CARS

Ford Mustang

Base Price: $25,585
Braking Distance: 119.1 feet
0-60 time: 5.3 seconds

Glossary

assembly line—a line of operations in a specific sequence that allows for quick and inexpensive assembly

baby boom—the period of time after World War II when a lot of babies were born

carburetor—the part of an engine where air and fuel are mixed to provide power

car culture—a love of cars that extends to lifestyle

crankshaft—a mechanical part that rotates the pistons in an engine

drag strips—straight, usually paved, tracks of roads used for drag racing

emissions—harmful substances that most automobiles release into the air

engine displacement—the total volume that pistons take up as they move through cylinders

fastback—style of car with a roof that slopes down in the back

horsepower—measurement of force used to gauge the power of engines

industry—a group of businesses that provide a particular service or product

internal combustion engines—the engines underneath the hoods of cars that run on gas

overhead valve V8 engine—a type of powerful engine where the cylinders are in a V shape

piston—a part in an engine that goes up and down to cause other parts to move

prosperous—successful

repurpose—to change the purpose of something

shocks—devices connected to wheels to reduce the effects of traveling on rough surfaces

torque—rotation that forces an engine's crankshaft to turn

transmissions—the parts that change a car's gears

Index

Beach Boys, The, 16, 22

Bullitt, 24

carburetor, 10, 18, 20

Carol & Cheryl, 18

Chevy Impala 409, 13–14, 16–18, 22, 24

Chrysler, 8

Chrysler C-300, 11

Detroit, 8, 18

Dodge Charger, 24–25

Ford, Henry, 6

Ford Model-T, 6

Ford Motor Company, 8, 24

Ford Mustang, 5, 15, 17, 22–26

General Motors (GM), 8–9 16, 18

horsepower, 10–11, 13–14, 16–17

internal combustion engines (ICE), 12

Jan and Dean, 18, 22

McQueen, Steve, 24

Oldsmobile Rocket 88, 10, 22

piston, 12–14, 16

Pontiac GTO, 17–19, 24

Ronny & the Daytonas, 18

Springsteen, Bruce, 22

torque, 14–15

transmissions, 8

V8 engine, 10, 16, 18, 26

World War II, 6

Answer Key

Let's Explore Math

page 5

1. independent: year; dependent: number of Mustangs

2. increased sharply 1964–1966 and then gradually declined.

page 7

1. In 1900, 0% of households owned cars.

2. The percent decreased.

3. Percents should be around 0, 2, 33, 45, 48, 65, 79, 82, and 86.

4. The graph shows trends over time.

page 9

A; D

page 15

1. An ascending line shows both cubic inches and power increasing.

2. An ascending line shows both displacement and torque increasing.

page 17

1.

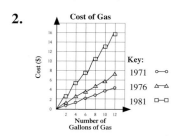

Horsepower and Quarter-Mile Times for Muscle Cars

2. In general, as horsepower increases, quarter-mile time decreases.

page 21

1. **1971:** $1.44, $2.16, $2.88, $3.60, $4.32; **1976:** $1.18, $3.54, $4.72, $5.90, $7.08; **1981:** $2.62, $5.24, $10.48, $13.10, $15.72

2.

Cost of Gas

Key:
1971 ○—○
1976 △—△
1981 □—□

3. **1971:** $0.36; **1976:** $0.59; **1981:** $1.31

4. **1971:** $c = 0.36n$; **1976:** $c = 0.59n$; **1981:** $c = 1.31n$

page 25

Equations may include $t = 14.5p$.

Problem Solving

Answers will vary but should include a recommended car with reasons and a table and graph showing depreciation.